SPARKLE CUPCAKES

The little black book

SPARKLE CUPCAKES

The little black book

KATHRYN SUTTON

CONTENTS

INTRODUCTION 9
BAKING WITH PASSION 11

BECAUSE IT'S MONDAY 13
PURE SPARKLE CUPCAKES 14

FAIRY PRINCESS MIA'S FIFTH BIRTHDAY PARTY 17
White Chocolate and Strawberry Cupcakes 19
MILK CHOCOLATE CUPCAKES 20

JOSH AND ELLIOTT'S MARDI GRAS PARTY 23
TWINKLE AND BLING CUPCAKES 24

LING FAMILY CHINESE NEW YEAR 27
Green Tea and Bubbles Cupcakes 28
Mandarin and Black Sesame Cupcakes 30
Fortune Cookies 31

STELLA'S VALENTINE'S DAY LOVE 33
Raspberry Red Velvet Cupcakes with Cream Cheese Frosting 34

MIKE AND BEC'S WEDDING BELLES 37
Oriental Flower Cupcakes 38
Lavender and Honey Cupcakes 41
Coconut Bling Cupcakes 42

ULTIMATE GIRLIE GATHERING 45
Ultimate Girlie Cupcakes 47
Spicy Lady 48

BROMANCE — 51
Salted Caramel Cupcakes — 52
Black Velvet Cupcakes — 55
Banana Toffee Cupcakes — 56

NIC'S BON VOYAGE PARTY — 59
Blueberry Cheesecake Cupcakes — 60
Big Apple and Cinnamon Cupcakes — 61

BETTY'S EASTER TREATS — 63
Triple Choc Cupcakes — 64
Dark Chocolate Marshmallow Cupcakes — 66

NANA AND MARTY MAKE CHRISTMAS TREATS — 69
Christmas Spice Cupcakes — 70
Peppermint Candy Cane Cupcakes — 72
Gingerbread Cookies — 73
Eggnogg Cupcakes — 76

MARTHA AND TOM'S MOTHER'S DAY CUPCAKES — 79
Lemon Daisy Cupcakes — 80
Shortbread Daisy Cookies — 83

TWEENS SUZI AND LOU'S SUMMER IN THE CITY — 87
Lime Cupcakes with Ginger Ice-cream — 88
Passionfruit Cupcakes with Blood Orange Sorbet — 89
Kumquat Cupcakes with Coconut Ice-cream — 90

JUDE'S NAMING DAY TEA PARTY — 93
Saffron and Coconut Sparkle Kisses — 94
Mango Jelly Dessert Shot — 96
Tzatziki and Cucumber Sandwich Slivers — 100
Chicken Waldorf Sandwich Swirls — 101
Mini Pistachio and Cardamom Cupcakes — 102
Orange Blossom Sparkle Kisses — 103

FIDO'S BIRTHDAY — 105
Pupcakes — 106
Doggie Birthday Cake — 107
Dog Biscuits — 108

ROCKSTAR GRANDMA — 111
Mandarin and Raspberry Trifle Celebration Cake — 112

FASHION FORWARD — 115
Fruit Skewers with Lavender Dipping Sauce — 116
The Skinny Cupcake — 117

PATCH OF GRASS — 119
Lamington Cupcakes — 120
Macadamia and Wattleseed Cupcakes — 121
Pavlova Cupcakes — 122

SPOOKY STUFF — 125
Pumpkin Spice Cupcakes — 126
Maple Syrup and Pecan Cupcakes — 129

SPRING CARNIVAL — 131
Bite-size Berry Cupcakes — 132

LITTLE BOY BLUE — 135
Afternoon Delight Cupcakes — 137

DECORATING — 138

ACKNOWLEDGEMENTS

The Little Black Book is a result of the amazing work of the talents of Sparkle staff—past and present. Nani Indah, our gifted and selfless pastry chef, deserves the accolades for many of her fabulous recipes in the following pages. Ngaire, who was there from day dot and Brian who helped us open the door on day one.

Each and every member of the Sparkle kitchen team, who have put their heart and soul into each cupcake they have baked or cake they created. To our fabulous front of house crew, who work tirelessly to make our store sparkle every day and strive to delight every customer.

Thank you to Con and Jonn, for sharing the dream.

Thank you to Diane, who wandered into Sparkle one day with the idea of creating this book, and the New Holland team, Karen, Kathy and Rochelle, who bought it to life.

Ultimately, we appreciate our customers—current and future—for who these recipes are created and who keep pushing us to new heights.

INTRODUCTION

Cupcakes are the Little Black Dress of the food world. Dress them up or down, they are comfortable for any occasion.

At Sparkle, it's our privilege to create cakes and cupcakes as the centerpiece for special occasions for our customers. We have made a 100th birthday cake and many a first birthday cupcake. Each wedding cake is thoughtfully and individually crafted. We have etched, piped and coloured to say 'Marry Me?' and 'Welcome to the World' on top of the little sugar bombs.

We send out stylish black and silver boxes and bags filled with Sparkle sugar treats across Sydney each day that cause a flurry at the reception desk of the most seasoned media agencies across town. Individual message tags carrying birthday wishes, lighting a new flame, or keeping a long-burning one alive with sweet sayings such as 'Let's make up over a cupcake'.

This *Little Black Book* of cupcakes captures some of the celebrations that have been marked with a Sparkle cupcake or many. Sparkle is about CELEBRATION. Capturing the moment, with the simplicity of a cupcake.

BAKING WITH PASSION

Baking is about chemistry and love—the right balance of great ingredients and some tender lovin' care as you bake and create! Enjoy!

ONLY THE BEST WILL DO
There are only a few ingredients in cupcakes, so it's important to use the very best quality. Don't compromise—particularly when it comes to flavoured oils, or beautiful syrups to give an exotic scent to the sweet treat.

For Sparkle recipes, we recommend:
- unsalted New Zealand butter
- plain flour
- fresh eggs—cage-free are a must and free-range or organic are a big plus
- caster sugar
- the very best quality vanilla—we love and use Heilala
- Monin syrups for their adventurous flavours

SIZE DOES MATTER
Classic size cupcakes should weigh 60 grams each, in a cupcake foil size 550.
    Mini cupcakes are 20 grams each and cupcake foil size 360. (Who would have thought that cupcake cases had numbers?)
    Be sure you have the right tray to fit your foil size. This is incredibly important for the shape of your final product.

CREAMIN' BABE
Seems simple, but this first step in the making of most cupcakes can make or break it! The butter and sugar must be creamed from yellow to a beautiful off-white colour. In summer, it may take only a few minutes while in winter, up to 20 minutes. Keep an eye on your batter at this stage.

LOVE THY OVEN

While we provide cooking estimates, you need to make friends with your oven. Get to know it. When you bring out your cooked cupcakes, they should be making a little sizzle sound. They are still bakin' away, but ready to come out.

THE RIGHT STUFF

Invest in good equipment. A great kitchen mixer will last you a lifetime. A set of scales is a must. A piping bag is required for many of the recipes and is also pretty handy to have in the kitchen drawer.

THE GOOD EGG

Eggs come in various sizes, from 50 grams through to 70 grams (1½–2oz). Here at Sparkle, we weigh our eggs and egg whites and recommend that you do too.

PRETTY TOPPINGS

Ready to Roll Icing (often called RTR but we prefer to call it Royal, because it sounds prettier), is available in big salami-like rolls at cake decorating stores and some supermarkets.

It is most commonly available in white, but is also found in black, red and an array of other colours. We recommend purchasing a little colour and creating your own shade.

RTR can be rolled out like pastry, using a rolling pin and a little cornflour to avoid sticking. Using a range of cutters, create fun shapes to decorate your little sugar bombs.

BUTTER CREAM

We don't recommend colouring butter cream icing. We use butter and because it's off-white, colours really don't take so well. It's also likely you won't achieve exactly the shade you require without a fair amount of trial and error.

EDIBLE GLITTER

Sparkle cupcakes often need a little twinkle and bling. Edible glitter is available from specialty cake decorating stores—it's well worth searching out!

So, get ready to put your hands in the flour. Be creative with your decorating and sparkle it up in the kitchen!

BECAUSE IT'S MONDAY

Life is about celebrating the moments. What's not to celebrate on a cold Monday afternoon? Fire up the oven, drag out that mixer and get bakin', because adding some Sparkle to your day can be for no particular reason at all.

PURE SPARKLE CUPCAKES

220g (7oz) butter
230g (7⅓ oz) caster sugar
205g (6½oz) eggs
330g (11oz) flour, sifted
12g (⅓ oz) baking powder
90ml (3⅓ fl oz) milk
10g (⅓ oz) vanilla bean paste

VANILLA FROSTING
115g (4oz) butter
310g (10oz) pure icing sugar
25g (⅔ oz) egg white (pasteurised)
½ teaspoon lemon juice
10g (⅓ oz) vanilla bean extract

Preheat oven to 145°C/275°F/Gas mark 1–2.

Cream butter and sugar on high speed in mixer until mixture is smooth and turns from yellow to off-white (between 5 and 20 minutes, depending on softness of butter).

Add eggs, one at a time, combining between additions. Do not let mixture split. Mix through until just combined. Do not overmix.

Sift flour and baking powder together. In a separate bowl, combine milk and vanilla bean paste. Add half the flour mixture and half the milk mixture to the butter mix. Mix well.

Add remaining sifted flour and baking powder, then remaining milk and vanilla bean paste. Mix until just combined.

Using an ice-cream scoop, spoon mixture into cupcake foils. Bake for 30 minutes, turning tray around once at 15 minutes.

VANILLA FROSTING
Whip butter until slightly pale and creamy. Add icing sugar and cream on high speed for further 5–10 minutes.

Add egg whites, lemon juice and vanilla bean extract. Cream an additional 3 minutes.

Spread on cooked cupcakes.

DECORATION
Silver sugar dot. See detail under 'Decorating'.

FAIRY PRINCESS MIA'S FIFTH BIRTHDAY PARTY

It's a precious age, when fairytales are real and an entire wardrobe is made up of tutus in different shades of pink. And it's a special celebration that warrants the creation of a birthday cake that whispers enchantment.

WHITE CHOCOLATE AND STRAWBERRY CUPCAKES

220g (7oz) butter
230g (7⅓ oz) caster sugar
205g (6½oz) eggs
330g (11oz) flour
12g (⅓oz) baking powder
90ml (3⅓fl oz) milk
10g (⅓oz) vanilla bean paste
100g (3½oz) strawberries, washed, hulled and chopped roughly
10ml (½fl oz) strawberry syrup
85g (3oz) white chocolate buds

STRAWBERRY SCENTED FROSTING
115g (4oz) butter
310g (10⅓oz) pure icing sugar
25g (¾oz) egg white (pasteurised)
½ teaspoon lemon juice
5ml (¼fl oz) strawberry syrup

Preheat oven to 145°C/275°F/Gas mark 1–2.

Cream butter and sugar on high speed in mixer until mixture turns from yellow to off-white (between 5 and 20 minutes, depending on softness of butter).

Add eggs, one at a time, combining between additions. Do not let mixture split. Mix through until just combined. Do not overmix.

Sift flour and baking powder together. In a separate bowl, combine milk and vanilla bean paste. Add half the flour mixture and half the milk mixture to the butter mixture. Fold in chopped strawberries and strawberry syrup.

Add remaining flour mixture and remaining milk mixture. Fold through white chocolate buds.

Using an ice-cream scoop, spoon mixture into cupcake foils. Bake for 30 minutes, turning tray around once at 15 minutes.

STRAWBERRY SCENTED FROSTING
Whip the butter until slightly pale and creamy. Then add icing sugar and cream on high speed for further 5–10 minutes.

Add egg whites, lemon juice and strawberry syrup. Cream an additional 3 minutes.

DECORATION
Use a piping bag with a round nozzle to pipe strawberry scented frosting on cooked cupckaes

Decorate with sugar fairy wings, sprinkled with edible glitter. See detail under Decorating.

MILK CHOCOLATE CUPCAKES

190g (6⅓oz) butter
200g (6½oz) caster sugar
190g (6⅓oz) eggs
95g (3oz) milk chocolate buds
105g (3½oz) sour cream
105ml (3½oz) buttermilk
40ml (2fl oz) oil
260g (8oz) plain flour
55g (1⅔oz) cocoa powder
8g (⅙oz) baking powder

BUTTER CREAM FROSTING
115g (4oz) butter
310g (10⅓oz) pure icing sugar
25g (⅔oz) egg white
½ teaspoon lemon juice
10ml (½fl oz) vanilla extract
180g (6oz) milk chocolate, melted

Preheat oven to 145°C/275°F/Gas mark 1-2.

Cream butter and sugar, using electric mixer, until light and fluffy. Mixture should turn from yellow to off-white.

Add half the eggs and half the oil. Stir until just combined. Add remaining eggs and oil gradually.

Combine chocolate buds, sour cream and buttermilk. Melt slowly in microwave or in a heatproof bowl set over simmering water. Mixture should be warm. Add oil to wet mixture and stir to combine.

Add wet mixture to butter mixture. Mixture will resemble a protein shake.

Combine flour, cocoa powder and baking powder in a separate bowl and then add to mixture.

Using an ice-cream scoop, spoon mixture into cupcake foils. Bake for 30 minutes, turning tray around once at 15 minutes.

BUTTER CREAM FROSTING
Cream butter and icing sugar on high speed in mixer (between 5 and 10 minutes, depending on softness of butter).

Add egg whites, lemon juice and vanilla bean extract. Cream for an additional 3 minutes. Mix in melted milk chocolate.

Spread on top of cooked cupcake.

DECORATION
Pile high with fairy floss.

JOSH AND ELLIOTT'S MARDI GRAS PARTY

Literally a parade of colour and life through city streets for a month on the summer calendar as a city celebrates diversity. Josh and Elliott have a gathering of friends during the official Mardi Gras parade, which snakes from the city centre up Oxford Street. In their luxurious apartment, overlooking the parade route, guests at Josh and Elliott's party are treated to a little sugar high.

TWINKLE AND BLING CUPCAKES

RAINBOW CAKE
220g (7oz) butter
230g (7⅓ oz) caster sugar
205g (6½oz) eggs
330g (11½oz) flour, sifted
12g (⅓oz) baking powder
90ml (3⅓fl oz) milk
10g (⅓oz) vanilla bean paste
5g (⅙oz) green powdered food colour
5g (⅙oz) yellow powdered food colour
5g (⅙oz) red powdered food colour

VANILLA FROSTING
115g (4oz) butter
310g (10⅓oz) pure icing sugar
25g egg white (pasteurised)
1 teaspoon lemon juice
10g (⅓oz) vanilla bean extract

RAINBOW CAKE
Preheat oven to 145°C/275°F/Gas mark 1–2.
　Cream butter and sugar on high speed in mixer until mixture turns from yellow to off-white in colour. This should be between 5 and 20 minutes, depending on softness of butter.
　Add eggs, one at a time, beating between additions to combine. Do not allow mixture to split. Mix through until just combined. Do not overmix.
　Sift flour and baking powder together. In a separate bowl, combine milk and vanilla bean paste. Add half flour mixture and half milk mixture to butter mixture. Mix well.
　Add remaining flour mixture, then remaining milk mixture. Mix well, then transfer mixture into 3 bowls.
　Add green food colour to bowl 1, yellow to bowl 2 and red to bowl 3.
　Using an ice-cream scoop, spoon mixture into cupcake foils. Bake for 30 minutes, turning tray around once at 15 minutes.

VANILLA FROSTING
Whip butter until slightly pale and creamy. Add icing sugar and cream on high speed for further 5–10 minutes, depending on softness of butter.
　Add egg whites, lemon juice and vanilla bean extract. Cream an additional 3 minutes.
　Spread over cooked cupcakes.

DECORATION
Cut sugar star shapes in bright rainbow colours. Mount on wire while still soft. Sprinkle with edible glitter. See detail under Decorating.

LING FAMILY
CHINESE NEW YEAR

Kung Hei Fat Choy—an occasion to herald the start of the first day of the lunar calendar. For Chinese families from Sydney to Shanghai, festivities centre around the Chinese themes of happiness, wealth and longevity. The Ling family bonds over some batter and butter cream to make these cupcakes to share with friends and relatives as they visit and are visited during the auspicious holiday season.

GREEN TEA AND BUBBLES CUPCAKES

220g (7oz) butter
230g (7⅓oz) caster sugar
205g (6½oz) eggs
330g (11oz) flour, sifted
12g (⅓oz) baking powder
90ml (3fl oz) milk
10g (⅓oz) vanilla bean paste
1 teaspoon maccha (powdered green tea)

BUBBLES FILLING
3 cups water
100g (3½oz) tapioca
100g (3½oz) sugar

Preheat oven to 145°C/275°F/Gas mark 1–2.

Using an electric mixer, cream butter and sugar on high speed until mixture turns from yellow to off-white. This should be between 5 and 20 minutes, depending on softness of butter.

Add eggs, one at a time, beating between additions. Do not allow mixture to split. Mix until just combined. Do not overmix.

Add half the sifted flour, half the baking powder, half the milk and half the vanilla bean paste. Stir to combine.

Add remaining sifted flour, baking powder, then remaining milk and vanilla bean paste. Fold in maccha.

Using an ice-cream scoop, spoon mixture into cupcake foils. Bake for 30 minutes, turning tray around once at 15 minutes.

BUBBLES FILLING
Bring water to boil in a saucepan. Once water is boiling, add tapioca, stirring so tapioca doesn't stick to the base.

Tapioca will become clear, with a small white dot in the middle. Add sugar and stir.

Cover saucepan and leave to simmer for 30 minutes, or until the white dot in the centre of tapioca has disappeared.

When they are cool enough to touch, use an apple-corer to remove centre of cupcakes. Fill each cupcake with 2 teaspoons of tapioca bubbles filling. Replace small piece of cake over filling to close hole.

LIME FROSTING

115g (3¾oz) butter
310g (10⅓oz) pure icing sugar
25g (¾oz) egg white (pasteurised)
½ teaspoon lemon juice
5ml (¼ fl oz) lime juice
several drops of lime oil

LIME FROSTING

Whip butter until slightly pale and creamy. Then add icing sugar and cream on high speed for further 5–10 minutes, depending on softness of butter.

Add egg whites, lemon juice, lime juice and lime oil. Cream an additional 3 minutes.

Spread over finished cupcakes.

DECORATION

Large sugar dots coloured orange and red. Use edible gold leaf to decorate. See detail under Decorating.

MANDARIN AND BLACK SESAME CUPCAKES

220g (7oz) butter
230g (7⅓oz) caster sugar
205g (6½oz) eggs
330g (11oz) flour, sifted
12g (½oz) baking powder
90ml (3⅓fl oz) milk
10g (⅓oz) vanilla bean paste
90g (3oz) tinned mandarin segments
100g (3½oz) black sesame seeds

MANDARIN TOPPING
115g (3¾oz) butter
310g (10⅓ oz) pure icing sugar
25g egg white (pasteurised)
1 teaspoon lemon juice
10ml (½fl oz) mandarin syrup

Preheat oven to 145°C/275°F/Gas mark 1–2.

Cream butter and sugar on high speed in mixer until mixture turns from yellow to off-white. This should be between 5 and 20 minutes, depending on softness of butter.

Add eggs, one at a time, combining between additions. Do not allow mixture to split. Mix until just combined. Do not overmix.

Sift flour and baking powder together. In a separate bowl, combine milk and vanilla bean paste. Add half flour mixture and half milk mixture to butter mixture. Mix well.

Add remaining flour mixture, then remaining milk mixture. Mix well.

Fold in mandarin segments and black sesame seeds. Bake for 30 minutes, turning tray around once at 15 minutes.

MANDARIN TOPPING
Whip butter until slightly pale and creamy. Add icing sugar and cream on high speed for further 5–10 minutes.

Add egg whites, lemon juice and mandarin syrup. Cream for an additional 3 minutes.

Spread over cooked cupcakes

DECORATION
Large orange and red coloured sugar dots. Use edible gold leaf to decorate. See detail in Decorating.

FORTUNE COOKIES

30g (1oz) egg white
70g (2⅓oz) caster sugar
pinch salt
dash of vanilla essence
45g (1½oz) plain flour, sifted

Write or type out your message on a small piece of paper. Preheat oven to 200°C/400°F/Gas mark 6.

Whisk egg white, caster sugar, salt and vanilla together until foamy. Add the flour and mix well. Place a teaspoon of the mixture on silicon paper. Using a spatula, spread the batter into rounds. Ensure the same thickness for even cooking.

Bake for 5 minutes or until golden. Quickly place the prepared message in the centre of the cookie. Bring two sides of the cookie together and then fold the cookie in half.

Place folded cookie into mini cupcake tray to dry out.

STELLA'S VALENTINE'S DAY LOVE

February 14 is a day to spread the love. Stella is baking from the heart, a once a year Sparkle Seasonal—the luscious Raspberry Red Velvet Cupcake with dribbly good cream cheese frosting. She's mixing up special treats for her true … loves, each Sealed With A Loving Kiss.

RASPBERRY RED VELVET CUPCAKES

220g (7oz) butter
230g (7⅓oz) caster sugar
205g (6½oz) eggs
330g (11oz) flour, sifted
12g (½oz) baking powder
90ml (3fl oz) milk
10g (½oz) vanilla bean paste
20g (⅔oz) dutch cocoa powder
½ teaspoon red powdered food colouring
15g (½oz) raspberry puree
150g (5oz) raspberries

CREAM CHEESE FROSTING
115g (3¾oz) butter
25g (1oz) cream cheese, softened
310g (10⅓oz) pure icing sugar
25g (1oz) egg white (pasteurised)
1 teaspoon lemon juice
10g (⅓oz) vanilla bean extract
pinch salt

Preheat oven to 145°C/275°F/Gas mark 1–2.

Using an electric mixer, cream butter and sugar on high speed until mixture turns from yellow to off-white. This should be between 5 and 20 minutes, depending on softness of butter.

Add eggs, one at a time, beating between additions. Do not allow mixture to split. Mix until just combined. Do not overmix.

Sift flour and baking powder together. In a separate bowl, combine milk and vanilla bean paste. Add half the flour mixture, then the dutch cocoa powder and red powdered food colouring. Add half the milk mixture, raspberry puree and raspberries.

Add remaining flour mixture and remaining milk mixture.

Using an ice-cream scoop, spoon mixture into cupcake foils. Bake for 30 minutes, turning tray around after 15 minutes.

CREAM CHEESE FROSTING
Whip butter until slightly pale and creamy. Add icing sugar and cream cheese and cream on high speed for further 5–10 minutes, depending on softness of butter.

Add egg whites, lemon juice, vanilla bean extract and salt. Cream an additional 3 minutes.

Spread on cooked cupcakes.

DECORATION
Decorate with sugar shapes, lips and hearts, coloured red. See detail under Decorating.

MIKE AND BEC'S WEDDING BELLES

Going to the chapel ... it's Mike and Bec's big day! The happy couple has chosen the most luscious and delicate cupcake flavours with a hint of floral for their special day, dazzling their guests with a little sparkle and bling.

ORIENTAL FLOWER CUPCAKES

220g (7oz) butter
230g (7⅓oz) caster sugar
205g (6oz) eggs
130g (4oz) flour, sifted
130g (4oz) rice flour, sifted
70g (2oz) ground almonds
12g (⅓oz) baking powder
90ml (3fl oz) milk
3 drops rose water
1 teaspoon rose syrup
100g (3½oz) lychees, chopped
10g (⅓oz) vanilla bean paste

ROSE WATER FROSTING
115g (4oz) butter
310g (10⅓oz) pure icing sugar
25g (⅔oz) egg white (pasteurised)
1 teaspoon lemon juice
3 drops rose water

Preheat oven to 145°C/275°F/Gas mark 1–2.

Cream butter and sugar on high speed in mixer for 5 to 20 minutes, depending on softness of butter. Mixture should turn from yellow to off-white.

Add eggs, one at a time, beating between additions. Do not allow mixture to split. Mix through until just combined. Do not overmix.

In a separate mixing bowl, combine the flours, almonds and baking powder. Add half this mixture to butter mixture and stir to combine.

In a separate mixing bowl, combine the milk, rose water and rose syrup, lychees and vanilla bean paste. Add half this mixture to the butter mixture and stir to combine.

Add remaining flour mixture, then remaining milk mixture. Using an ice-cream scoop, spoon mixture into cupcake foils.

Bake for 30 minutes, turning tray around once at 15 minutes.

ROSE WATER FROSTING
Whip butter until slightly pale and creamy. Add icing sugar and cream on high speed for further 5–10 minutes, depending on softness of butter.

Add egg whites, lemon juice and rose water. Cream an additional 3 minutes.

Spread over cooked cupcakes.

DECORATION
Cover frosting with a large circle of plastic icing. Decorate with sugar dot, sprinkled with edible glitter. See detail in Decorating.

LAVENDER AND HONEY CUPCAKES

220g (7oz) butter
230g (7⅓oz) caster sugar
205g (6oz) eggs
330g (11oz) flour
12g (⅓oz) baking powder
90ml (3fl oz) milk
10g (⅓oz) vanilla bean paste
½ teaspoon edible lavender oil

HONEY FROSTING
115g (4oz) butter
310g (10⅓oz) pure icing sugar
25g egg white (pasturised)
1 teaspoon lemon juice
2 drops edible lavender oil
6g (⅙oz) french-style lavender honey

Preheat oven to 145°C/275°F/Gas mark 1–2.
 Cream butter and sugar on high speed in mixer for 5 to 20 minutes, depending on softness of butter. Mixture should turn from yellow to off-white.
 Add eggs, one at a time, beating between additions. Do not allow mixture to split.
 In a separate mixing bowl, sift flour and baking powder together. Add half this mixture to butter mixture and stir to combine.
 In another mixing bowl, combine milk, vanilla bean paste and lavender oil. Pour half this mixture into the butter mixture and stir to combine. Add remaining flour mixture and milk mixture to butter mixture and stir until fully combined.
 Mix until just combined. Do not overmix.
 Using an ice-cream scoop, spoon mixture into cupcake foils. Bake for 30 minutes, turning tray around once at 15 minutes.

HONEY FROSTING
Whip butter until slighly pale and creamy. Add icing sugar and cream on high speed in mixer for further 5–10 minutes.
 Add egg whites, lemon juice, lavender oil and honey. Cream for an additional 3 minutes.
 Spread over cooked cupcakes.

DECORATION
Cover frosting with a large circle of plastic icing smoothened over. See detail under Decorating.

COCONUT BLING CUPCAKES

220g (7oz) butter
230g (7⅓oz) caster sugar
205g (6oz) eggs
330g (11oz) flour, sifted
12g (⅓oz) baking powder
90ml (3fl oz) milk
4 drops coconut essence
10g (⅓oz) vanilla bean paste
50ml (1¾fl oz) coconut cream
50g (1⅔oz) desiccated coconut

COCONUT ICE FROSTING
300g (11oz) shredded coconut
40g (1⅓oz) butter, melted
375g (12½oz) pure icing sugar
pinch salt
60ml (2fl oz) coconut cream

Preheat oven to 145°C/275°F/Gas mark 1–2.
Using electric beaters, cream butter and sugar on high speed for 5 to 20 minutes, depending on softness of butter. Mixture should turn from yellow to off-white.
Add eggs, one at a time, beating between additions. Do not allow mixture to split.
Sift flour and baking powder together. Add half of this to butter mixture and stir to combine.
In another bowl, combine milk, coconut essence and vanilla bean paste. Add half of this to butter mixture and stir to combine.
Add remaining flour mixture and milk mixture to butter mixture and stir until fully combined.
Fold in coconut cream and desiccated coconut. Using an ice-cream scoop, spoon mixture into cupcake foils.
Bake for 30 minutes, turning tray around once at 15 minutes.

COCONUT ICE FROSTING
In a frypan on low heat, toast shredded coconut until light brown. Be careful not to burn the coconut.
In a large bowl, mix remaining ingredients for about 5 minutes until smooth.
Spread over cooked cupcakes, roll in dessicated coconut and sprinkle with edible glitter, if desired.

ULTIMATE GIRLIE GATHERING

The girls are getting together over cocktails and cupcakes, all frocked up and ready for a night on the town. There are lots of giggles and high-volume chatter about the important things in life—shopping, shoes and boys!

ULTIMATE GIRLIE CUPCAKES

220g (7oz) butter
230g (7⅓oz) caster sugar
205g (6oz) eggs
330g (11oz) flour, sifted
12g (1oz) baking powder
90ml (3fl oz) milk
10ml (⅓fl oz) strawberry syrup
3 drops red colouring
10g (⅓oz) vanilla bean paste
100g (3½oz) strawberries

CREAM CHEESE FROSTING
115g (4oz) butter
25g (⅔oz) cream cheese, softened
310g (10⅓oz) pure icing sugar
25g (⅔oz) egg white (pastur–ised)
1 teaspoon lemon juice
pinch salt

Preheat oven to 145°C/275°F/Gas mark 1–2.

Using an electric beater, cream butter and sugar on high speed for 5 to 20 minutes, depending on softness of butter. Mixture should turn from yellow to off-white.

Add eggs, one at a time, beating between additions. Do not allow mixture to split. Mix until just combined. Do not overmix.

Combine flour and baking powder. In a separate bowl, combine milk, strawberry syrup, food colouring and vanilla bean paste. Add half the flour mixture and half the milk mixture to butter mixture and stir to combine.

Add remaining flour mixture and remaining milk mixture to butter mixture and stir until fully combined. Fold in strawberries.

Using an ice-cream scoop, spoon mixture into cupcake foils. Bake for 30 minutes, turning tray around once at 15 minutes.

CREAM CHEESE FROSTING
Whip butter until slightly pale and creamy. Add cream cheese and icing sugar and cream on high speed for further 5–10 minutes.

Add egg whites, lemon juice and salt. Cream an additional 3 minutes.

DECORATION
Using a piping bag fitted with a plain nozzle, pipe frosting over cooked cupcakes. Top with pink sugar shoe shape. See Decorating for details.

SPICY LADY

190g (6¼oz) butter
200g (6½oz) caster sugar
190g (6¼oz) eggs
40ml (1½fl oz) oil
95g (3oz) milk chocolate buds
105ml (3½fl oz) buttermilk
105g (3½oz) sour cream
260g (8¼oz) plain flour
55g (1¾oz) cocoa powder
8g (⅓oz) baking powder
20 crushed pink peppercorns

MILK CHOCOLATE GANACHE
100g (3½oz) pure cream
175g (5¾oz) couverture milk chocolate
35g (1oz) butter
5g crushed pink peppercorns

Preheat oven to 145°C/275°F/Gas mark 1–2.

Using electric beaters, cream butter and sugar until light and fluffy. Mixture should turn from yellow to off-white. Add half eggs and half oil. Mix until just combined. Add remaining eggs and oil gradually. In a microwave or heatproof bowl set over a pot of simmering water, gently melt chocolate buds in buttermilk with sour cream. Mixture should be warm, around 50°C/100°F.

Sift the flour, cocoa and baking powder together in a medium bowl. Add half this mixture and half the melted chocolate mixture to the butter mixture. Gently combine then add remaining flour mixture and chocolate mixture and beat until mixture is combined. Fold peppercorns through the batter.

Using an ice-cream scoop, spoon batter into cupcake foils.

Bake for 30 minutes, turning tray around once at 15 minutes.

MILK CHOCOLATE GANACHE
Heat cream on low heat until just boiling. Remove from heat, pour over chocolate and stir. Add butter.

Fold in crushed pink peppercorns.

Dip cooked cupcake in topping and allow to dry for smooth, glossy finish.

BROMANCE

Real men eat cupcakes. The game is on the box. Meat pies, beer and yes, cupcakes. Here are three favourite man-cakes.

SALTED CARAMEL CUPCAKES

....

CARAMEL SAUCE
500g (1lb) caster sugar
70g (2⅓oz) butter
825ml (27½fl oz) fresh cream
½ teaspoon sea salt

CARAMEL CUPCAKES
220g (7oz) butter
230g (7⅓oz) caster sugar
205g (6oz) eggs
330g (11oz) flour
12g (⅓oz) baking powder
90ml (3fl oz) milk
10g (⅓oz) vanilla bean paste
50ml (1¾fl oz) caramel sauce (see above)

CARAMEL SAUCE
Stir about 200 grams of sugar in a saucepan on low heat until melted. Add another 200 grams and then the final 100 grams.

Continue to cook, stirring continuously. Do not allow mixture to burn. Once all sugar has dissolved, add the butter and continue to stir.

In a separate saucepan, lightly warm the fresh cream. Do not boil. Add the cream gradually into the sugar mixture and continue stirring until mixture is smooth. It should be about 115°C/250°F if measuring with a sugar thermometer.

CARAMEL CUPCAKES
Preheat oven to 145°C/275°F/Gas mark 1–2.

Using electric beaters, cream butter and sugar on high speed in mixer for 5 to 20 minutes, depending on softness of butter. Mixture should turn from yellow to off-white.

Add eggs, one at a time, beating between additions. Do not allow mixture to split.

Sift together flour and baking powder. In a separate bowl, combine milk and vanilla bean paste. Add half the flour mixture and half the milk mixture to the butter mixture and stir to combine.

Add remaining flour mixture and milk mixture to butter mixture and stir until fully combined. Fold in caramel sauce.

Using an ice-cream scoop, spoon mixture into cupcake foils. Bake for 30 minutes, turning tray around once at 15 minutes.

When cupcakes cool enough to touch, use an apple corer to remove the centre of each cupcake.

Fill each cupcake with two teaspoons of caramel sauce. Replace a small piece of cake on top of the caramel sauce to seal.

CARAMEL FROSTING
115g (4oz) butter
310g (10⅓oz) pure icing sugar
25g (¾oz) egg white (pasturised)
½ teaspoon lemon juice
50ml (1¾fl oz) caramel sauce
10g (⅓oz) vanilla bean extract

CARAMEL FROSTING
Whip butter until slightly pale and creamy. Add icing sugar and cream on high speed in mixer for further 5 to 10 minutes, depending on softness of butter.

Add egg whites, lemon juice, caramel sauce and vanilla bean extract. Cream an additional 3 minutes.

DECORATION
Using a piping bag with a large round nozzle, pipe frosting on top of cooked cupcakes.

Top with a patterned chocoalte disk from a transfer sheet. See details in Decorating.

BLACK VELVET CUPCAKES

290g (9¼oz) butter
265g (8½oz) dark chocolate
200g (6½oz) caster sugar
135g (4⅓oz) egg
255g (8oz) plain flour
35g (1⅙oz) dutch cocoa powder
10g (⅓oz) baking powder

DARK CHOCOATE GANACHE
75g (2½oz) dark chocolate
65g (2oz) pure cream

Preheat oven to 90°C/200°F/Gas mark 1.
　Melt butter in a heatproof bowl set over boiling water. Add chocolate and sugar.
　Whisk for 30 seconds. Add eggs and whisk for further 30 seconds.
　Add remaining ingredients and whisk for 1 minute.
　Bake for 45 minutes, turning after 25 minutes.

DARK CHOCOATE GANACHE
Heat cream in a saucepan on medium heat until almost boiling.
　Break chocolate into a heatproof bowl. Pour near boiling cream over chocolate and stir until smooth.

DECORATION
Using a piping bag with a large, round nozzle, pipe a large dollop of slightly cooled ganache on top of cooked cupcake.
　Top with patterned chocolate disk from chocolate transfer sheet. See details in Decorating.

BANANA TOFFEE CUPCAKES

TOFFEE SAUCE
250g (8oz) can condensed milk

BANANA CUPCAKE
255g (8⅒oz) butter
265g (7oz) brown sugar
5g (⅙oz) vanilla bean paste
265g (7oz) eggs
355g (11½oz) plain flour
13g (⅓oz) baking powder
pinch baking soda
pinch salt
55g (1⅔oz) over-ripe banana, mashed
100ml (3½fl oz) milk

TOFFEE SAUCE
Place unopened tin of condensed milk in a saucepan. Cover tin with water and bring to the boil. Boil for at least 90 minutes, topping up water to ensure tin is completely covered. Allow to cool before opening.

BANANA CUPCAKE
Preheat oven to 145°C/275°F/Gas mark 1–2.
    Cream butter and sugar for about 3 minutes, until mixture is just combined. Slowly add the eggs, beating between additions to avoid the mixture splitting and separating.
    In a large bowl, sift together flour, baking powder, baking soda and salt. In a separate bowl, mash banana and milk until it forms a paste.
    Add half the flour mixture to the butter mixture, then half the banana and milk mixture. Mix thoroughly. Add remaining flour mixture and remaining banana and milk. Mix until fully combined.
    Using an ice-cream scoop, spoon mixture into cupcake foils. Bake for 30 minutes, turning tray around once at 15 minutes.
    When they are cool enough to touch, use an apple corer to remove centre of cupcakes. Fill each cupcake with two teaspoons of toffee sauce. Replace a small piece of cake on top of toffee to seal.

TOFFEE FROSTING
115g (4oz) butter
310g (10⅔oz) pure icing sugar
25g (⅔oz) egg white (pasteurised)
½ teaspoon lemon juice
10g (⅓oz) vanilla bean extract
50g (1⅔oz) toffee sauce (see above)

TOFFEE FROSTING
Whip the butter until slightly pale and creamy. Add icing sugar and cream on high speed for further 5 to 10 minutes.
 Add egg whites, lemon juice and vanilla bean extract. Cream an additional 3 minutes.

DECORATION
Using a piping bag with a large round nozzle, pipe a large dollop of buttercream on top of cupcake. Top with chocolate disk with pattern from chocolate transfer sheet. See detail in Decorating.

NIC'S NYC BON VOYAGE

Nic's going to NYC—The Big Apple and the birthplace of the modern cupcake. She's scored a fabulous job in advertising and couldn't be more excited. She's having a gathering with friends and family to say farewells, and to plan their visits in her diary so her sofa couch isn't double booked! Nothing's more American than apple and cinnamon—except maybe blueberry cheesecake.

BLUEBERRY CREAM CHEESE CUPCAKES

220g (7oz) butter
230g (7½oz) caster sugar
205g (6½oz) eggs
330g (11oz) flour
12g (⅓oz) baking powder
90ml (3fl oz) milk
10g (⅓oz) vanilla bean paste
125g (4oz) blueberries, chopped
10g (⅓oz) blueberry syrup

CREAM CHEESE FROSTING
115g (3¾oz) butter
25g (⅔oz) cream cheese, softened
310g (10⅓oz) pure icing sugar
25g (⅔oz) egg white (pasteurised)
1 teaspoon lemon juice
10g (⅓oz) vanilla bean extract
pinch salt

Preheat oven to 145°C/275°F/Gas mark 2.

Using an electric mixer on high speed, cream butter and sugar until mixture turns from yellow to off-white. This should be between 5 and 20 minutes, depending on softness of butter. Add eggs, one at a time, beating between additions. Do not allow mixture to split.

Sift together the flour and baking powder. In a separate bowl, combine milk and vanilla bean paste.

And half the flour mixture and half the milk mixture to the butter mixture, then add blueberries and blueberry syrup.

Add remaining flour mixture, then remaining milk mixture. Using an ice-cream scoop, spoon batter into cupcake foils. Bake for 30 minutes, turning tray around once at 15 minutes.

CREAM CHEESE FROSTING
Whip the butter and cream cheese until pale and creamy.

Add icing sugar and beat on high speed for further 5–10 minutes. Add egg whites, lemon juice, vanilla bean extract and salt. Beat for an additional 3 minutes.

Spread over cooked cupcakes

BIG APPLE AND CINNAMON CUPCAKES

220g (7oz) butter
230g (7⅓oz) caster sugar
205g (6¾oz) eggs
330g (11oz) flour
12g (⅓oz) baking powder
90ml (3fl oz) milk
10g (⅓oz) vanilla bean paste

SUGAR SYRUP
100g (3½oz) caster sugar
100ml (3½fl oz) water

SUGAR CINNAMON DUST
100g (3½oz) caster sugar
50g (1½oz) cinnamon, ground

Preheat oven to 145°C/275°F/Gas mark 1–2.

Using electric beaters, cream butter and sugar on high speed for 5 to 20 minutes, depending on softness of butter. Mixture should turn from yellow to off-white.

Add eggs, one at a time, beating between additions. Do not allow mixture to split. Mix until just combined. Do not over mix.

Sift flour and baking powder together. In a separate bowl, combine milk and vanilla bean paste.

Add half the flour mixture and half the milk mixture to the butter mixture. Mix well.

Add remaining flour mixture and then remaining milk and vanilla bean paste. Mix well.

Using an ice-cream scoop, spoon mixture into cupcake foils. Bake for 30 minutes, turning tray around once at 15 minutes.

SUGAR SYRUP
Boil sugar in water, stirring until dissolved.

DECORATION
As soon as cupcakes come out of the oven, brush with sugar syrup and then dip cupcakes in sugar cinnamon dust. Cut letters 'N', 'Y' and 'C' out of green-coloured sugar shapes.

BETTY'S EASTER TREATS

Easter seems to be the official holiday for chocolate—we're talking food, not religion. It's a time to celebrate all things bright, new and fluffy. Betty's been a-bakin' some chocolate treats to take in to the office nd share around. BIG brownie points all round!

TRIPLE CHOCOLATE CUPCAKES

220g (7oz) butter
230g (7⅓oz) caster sugar
205g (6½oz) eggs
330g (11oz) flour
12g (⅓oz) baking powder
90ml (3fl oz) milk
10g (⅓oz) vanilla bean paste
50g (1¾oz) white chocolate buds
50g (1¾oz) milk chocolate buds
50g (1¾oz) dark chocolate buds

MILK CHOCOLATE FROSTING
115g (4oz) butter
310g (10⅓oz) pure icing sugar
25g (⅔oz) egg white (pasteurised)
½ teaspoon lemon juice
10g (⅓oz) vanilla bean extract
180g (6oz) milk chocolate buds, melted

Preheat oven to 145°C/275°F/Gas mark 1–2.
 Cream butter and sugar on high speed in mixer for between 5 and 20 minutes, depending on softness of butter. Mixture should turn from yellow to off-white.
 Add eggs, one at a time, beating between additions. Do not allow mixture to split.
 In a medium bowl, sift flour and baking powder together. In a separate bowl, combine milk and vanilla bean paste.
 Add half the flour mixture and half the milk mixture to the butter mixture. Mix well.
 Add remaining flour mixture and remaining milk mixture to butter mixture. Mix well. Fold in combined chocolate buds.
 Using an ice-cream scoop, spoon mixture into cupcake foils. Bake for 30 minutes, turning tray around once at 15 minutes.

MILK CHOCOLATE FROSTING
Using electric beaters, cream butter and icing sugar on high speed for 5 to 10 minutes, depending on softness of butter.
 Add egg whites, lemon juice, vanilla bean extract and melted chocolate. Cream an additional 3 minutes.
 Spread over cooked cupcakes

DECORATION
Cover cupcakes with chocolate butter cream frosting. Roll in chocolate shavings. Decorate with yellow chick sugar shape.
 For three different frostings, use the same recipe and replace milk chocolate buds with white and dark chocolate.

DARK CHOCOLATE MARSHMALLOW CUPCAKES

290g (10oz) butter
385ml (12½oz) water
265g (8½oz) dark chocolate
200g (6½oz) caster sugar
135g (4¼oz) eggs
255g (8oz) plain flour
35g (1oz) dutch cocoa powder
10g (⅓oz) baking powder
50 chopped marshmallows

DARK CHOCOLATE GANACHE
100g (3½oz) pure cream
125g (4oz) dark chocolate
35g (1¼oz) butter
mini marshmallows, to decorate

Preheat oven to 90°C/200°F/Gas mark 1.
    Melt butter in a large saucepan and add water, chocolate and sugar. Whisk for 30 seconds.
    Add eggs and whisk for further 30 seconds. Sift together remaining ingredients and add to butter mixture. Whisk for a further 1 minute.
    Using an ice-cream scoop, spoon mixture into cupcake foils and bake for 45 minutes, turning after 25 minutes.

DARK CHOCOLATE GANACHE
Bring cream to the boil. Remove from heat and pour over chocolate. Stir, then add butter. Stir until butter and chocolate melt and mixture is smooth.
    Top with mini marshmallows.

CHRISTMAS CHEER

The holiday season is a time for family and friends, and it's time for Nana to teach grandson Marty a few tricks in the kitchen. They put their hands in the flour together and make yummy treats for the rest of the family. They wrap them up in a beautiful box Marty picked himself, with some extra glitter and sparkle because it's Christmas, and then watch the smiles of joy on Christmas Day. as the box is unwrapped. There's nothing quite like a gift made from the heart.

CHRISTMAS SPICE CUPCAKES

260g (8⅓oz) butter
270g (8⅔oz) caster sugar
250g (8oz) eggs
390g (12½oz) flour
14g (½oz) baking powder
½ teaspoon cinnamon
1 teaspoon mixed spice
2 teaspoons nutmeg
110g (3¾oz) milk
10g (⅓oz) vanilla bean paste
500g (1lb) dried fruit

BRANDY BUTTER CREAM
115g (4oz) butter
310g (10⅓oz) pure icing sugar
25g (1oz) egg white, pasteurised
½ teaspoon lemon juice
10g (⅓oz) vanilla bean extract
10ml (⅓fl oz) brandy

Preheat oven to 140–160°C/275–325°F/Gas mark 1–3 (oven temperature may vary, depending on your oven type).

Using electric beaters, cream butter and sugar on high speed for 5 to 20 minutes, depending on softness of butter.

Add eggs, one at a time, beating between additions. Do not allow mixture to split. Mix until just combined. Do not over mix.

In a medium bowl, sift flour and baking powder together. Add cinnamon, mixed spice and nutmeg. In a separate bowl, combine milk and vanilla bean paste.

Add half the flour mixture and half the milk mixture to the butter mixture. Mix well.

Add remaining flour mixture and milk mixture to butter mixture. Mix thoroughly until batter is smooth. Fold in dried fruit.

Using an ice-cream scoop, spoon batter into foils. Bake for 30 minutes, turning tray around at 15 minutes.

BRANDY BUTTER CREAM
Whip butter until slightly pale and creamy. Add icing sugar and cream on high speed for 5 to 10 minutes, depending on softness of butter.

Add egg whites, lemon juice and vanilla bean extract. Cream an additional 3 minutes.

Spread over cooked cupcakes.

DECORATION
Decorate with a sugar silver or red coloured snowflake shape. See detail in Decorating.

PEPPERMINT CANDY CANE CUPCAKES

190g (6¼oz) butter
200g (6½oz) caster sugar
190g (6¼oz) eggs
95g (3¼oz) milk chocolate buds
105ml (3½fl oz) buttermilk
50g (1¾oz) sour cream
3 drops edible peppermint oil
260g (8¼oz) plain flour
55g (2oz) cocoa powder
8g (⅓oz) baking powder

TOPPING
115g (4oz) butter
310g (10⅓oz) pure icing sugar
25g (¾oz) egg white, pasteurised
½ teaspoon lemon juice
10g (⅓oz) vanilla bean extract
180g (6oz) milk chocolate, melted
50g (1⅔oz) candy cane, crushed into crumbs

Preheat oven to 140–160°C/275–325°F/Gas mark 1–3 (temperature may vary, depending on your oven type).

Using electric beaters, cream butter and sugar until light and fluffy. Mixture should turn from yellow to off-white. Add eggs all at once. Continue mixing until mixture is fully combined and smooth.

In a microwave or a heatproof bowl set over a pot of simmering water, gently melt chocolate buds in buttermilk with sour cream. Mixture should be warm, around 50°C/100°F. Add peppermint oil to chocolate mixture.

Add chocolate mixture to butter mixture. It should resemble a protein shake.

In a medium bowl, sift flour, cocoa powder and baking powder together. Add to butter mixture and stir until well combined.

Bake for 30 minutes, turning tray around at 15 minutes.

TOPPING
Using electric beaters, cream butter and icing sugar on high speed in mixer for 5 to 10 minutes, depending on softness of butter.

Add egg whites, lemon juice and vanilla bean extract. Cream for an additional 3 minutes. Stir in melted milk chocolate. Cool slightly. Mix through crushed candy cane.

Spread on cooked cupcakes.

GINGERBREAD COOKIES

200g (6½oz) butter
200g (6½oz) brown sugar
160g (5½oz) honey
100g (3½oz) eggs
625g (20⅔oz) flour
5g (¼oz) salt
5g (¼oz) bicarbonate soda
5g (¼oz) ground ginger
pinch cinnamon
pinch nutmeg
10g (⅓oz) mixed spice
14g (½oz) baking powder

TOPPING
250g (8oz) pure icing sugar
25g (⅔oz) egg white, pasteurised
½ teaspoon lemon juice

Using electric beaters, cream butter and sugar on high speed in mixer until it turns from bright yellow to pale yellow.

Add honey and eggs, one at a time, beating between additions. Do not allow mixture to split.

In a mixing bowl, sift together remaining ingredients. Add half this mixture to the butter mixture. Mix well, then add remaining half of dry ingredients. Mix until batter is just combined.

Preheat oven to 100°C/200°F/Gas mark 1. Using your hands, work the dough on the bench until it comes together. It will break and look a little dry.

Roll out dough and allow to rest in the fridge for about 20 minutes. Using a cookie cutter, cut into shapes and lay on a greased baking tray. Bake for 8 minutes, turn and bake for another 4 minutes, depending on the size and shape of cookies.

TOPPING
Cream icing sugar and egg white with lemon juice on high speed in mixer for 5 to 10 minutes, depending on softness of butter.

Pipe and spread icing on baked cookies.

EGGNOG CUPCAKES

260g (8⅓oz) butter
270g (8⅔oz) caster sugar
250g (8oz) eggs
390g (11¾oz) flour
14g (½oz) baking powder
1 teaspoon ground cinnamon
½ teaspoon ground nutmeg
110ml (3½fl oz) milk
10g (⅓oz) vanilla bean paste
10ml (⅓oz) rum

EGGNOG
100g (3½oz) custard powder
150ml (5fl oz) milk
pinch nutmeg, ground
pinch cinnamon, ground
10ml (⅓fl oz) rum

Preheat oven to 140–160°C/275–325°F/Gas mark 1–3 (oven temperature may vary, depending on your oven type).

Using electric beaters, cream butter and sugar on high speed for 5 to 20 minutes, depending on softness of butter.

Add eggs, one at a time, beating between additions. Do not allow mixture to split. Mix until just combined. Do not over mix.

In a medium bowl, sift flour and baking powder together. Add cinnamon and nutmeg. In a separate bowl, combine milk, vanilla bean paste and rum.

Add half the flour mixture and half the milk mixture to the butter mixture. Stir until combined.

Add remaining flour mixture and remaining milk mixture to butter mixture. Mix thoroughly to combine until mixture is a smooth batter.

Using an ice-cream scoop, spoon batter into cupcake foils. Bake for 30 minutes, turning tray around at 15 minutes.

EGGNOG
In a saucepan on low heat, combine custard powder, sugar and milk. Stir until powder and sugar dissolves. Add nutmeg and cinnamon. Slowly bring to the boil.

Once mixture has boiled and thickened, remove from heat and add rum. Cover custard with cling wrap to avoid forming a skin. This is best made the day before and refrigerated overnight.

When cupcakes are cool enough to handle, use an apple corer to remove centre of cupcakes. Use two teaspoons to fill each cupcake with eggnog. Replace a small piece of cake over the top eggnog to seal.

BUTTER CREAM TOPPING
115g (4oz) butter
310g (10⅓oz) pure icing sugar
25g (⅔oz) egg white
½ teaspoon lemon juice
1 teaspoon vanilla extract

BUTTER CREAM TOPPING
Whip butter until slightly pale and creamy. Add icing sugar and cream on high speed for further 5 to 10 minute.

Add egg whites, lemon juice and vanilla extract. Cream an additional 3 minutes.

Spread over cooked cupcakes.

DECORATION
Decorate with sugar snowflake shape, coloured silver or red.

MARTHA AND TOM'S MOTHER'S DAY CUPCAKES

It's time for twins Martha and Tom to let Mum know how much they love her, despite all the trouble the mischievous duo often cause. With some sugar and spice (under Dad's direction to make sure the kitchen isn't destroyed) the twins will make Mum melt with their homemade gift.

LEMON DAISY CUPCAKES

LEMON BUTTER
300ml (10fl oz) lemon juice
300g (10oz) caster sugar
9 eggs, lightly beaten
300g (10oz) butter

LEMON MYRTLE BATTER
220g (7oz) butter
230g (7⅓oz) caster sugar
205g (6½oz) eggs
330g (11oz) flour
12g (⅓oz) baking powder
90ml (3fl oz) milk
10g (⅓oz) vanilla bean paste
10g (⅓oz) lemon butter
5g (¹⁄₅oz) ground lemon myrtle

MERINGUE TOPPING
150g (5oz) caster sugar
1 egg white, pasteurised

LEMON BUTTER
In a heatproof bowl set over a pot of simmering water, boil lemon juice and caster sugar. Slowly add whisked eggs and cook gently while stirring. Remove from heat and add butter, stirring until butter is melted.

LEMON MYRTLE BATTER
Preheat oven to 145°C/275°F/Gas mark 1–2.

Using electric beaters, cream butter and sugar on high speed in mixer for 5 to 20 minutes, depending on softness of butter. Mixture should turn from yellow to off-white.

Add eggs, one at a time, beating between additions. Do not allow mixture to split. Mix until just combined. Do not over mix.

In a medium mixing bowl, sift flour and baking powder together. In another bowl, combine milk and vanilla bean paste.

Add half the flour mixture and half the milk mixture to the butter and sugar mixture. Combine well and then add remaining flour mixture and remaining milk mixture. Mix well. Fold in lemon butter and lemon myrtle.

Using an ice-cream scoop, spoon mixture into cupcake foils. Bake for 30 minutes, turning tray around once at 15 minutes.

When they are cool enough to handle, use an apple corer to remove centre of cupcakes. Fill each cupcake with two teaspoons of lemon butter. Replace a small piece of cake over the top to close the hole.

SHORTBREAD DAISY COOKIES

80g (2⅔oz) caster sugar
1 teaspoon vanilla paste
200g (6½oz) unsalted butter
100g (3½oz) rice flour
pinch salt
200g (6½oz) plain flour

Preheat oven to 160°C/325°F/Gas mark 2–3.

Combine sugar, vanilla paste and butter in a bowl. Using a spatula, mix until just combined.

Add remaining ingredients and mix until just combined. Do not overmix.

On a floured surface, roll out dough to desired thickness.

Using a daisy-shaped cutter, cut dough into shapes and transfer into a baking paper-lined tray.

Bake for 15 to 20 minutes.

TWEENS SUZI AND LOU'S SUMMER IN THE CITY

Summertime. Jumping in the neighbour's pool after school until Mum or Dad is screeching over the fence to come home. Carefree and full of energy. Long summer afternoons with your best friend in the whole wide world. Here's a special summer treat—just out of the oven—naked cupcakes stuffed with cooling homemade ice-cream.

LIME CUPCAKES WITH GINGER ICE-CREAM

220g (7oz) butter
230g (7⅓oz) caster sugar
205g (6½oz) eggs
330g (11oz) flour
12g (13oz) baking powder
90ml (3fl oz) milk
10g (⅓oz) vanilla bean paste
2 drops lime oil
5g (⅙oz) fresh lime zest

GINGER ICE-CREAM
500ml (16fl oz) full cream milk
1 teaspoon vanilla paste
pinch salt
1 teaspoon ground ginger
125g (4oz) egg yolk
175g (6oz) caster sugar
250ml (8fl oz) double cream
30g (1oz) molasses

Preheat oven to 145°C/275°F/Gas mark 1–2.

Using electric beaters, cream butter and sugar on high speed for 5 to 20 minutes, depending on softness of butter. Mixture should turn from yellow to off-white.

Add eggs, one at a time, beating between additions. Do not allow mixture to split. Mix until just combined. Do not overmix.

Sift flour and baking powder together. In a separate bowl, combine milk and vanilla bean paste. Add half the flour mixture, half the milk mixture and the lime oil to the butter and sugar mixture. Combine well and then add remaining flour mixture and remaining milk mixture. Fold in lime zest.

Use an ice-cream scoop to spoon batter into cupcake foils. Bake for 30 minutes, turning tray around once at 15minutes.

GINGER ICE-CREAM
Bring milk, vanilla paste, salt and ground ginger to the boil.

Combine egg and sugar in a large bowl and beat until sugar is dissolved. Pour a third of boiling milk mixture into the egg yolk mixture, whisking continuously to prevent the egg from cooking.

Pour the egg yolk mixture back into the saucepan and turn the heat down to low. Keep stirring so that mixture does not stick to the bottom of the saucepan.

Cook until mixture coats the back of a spoon. Stir in the double cream and molasses. Refrigerate overnight and process using an ice-cream maker.

DECORATION
Scoop ice-cream on top of cupcake. Top with fresh lemon zest.

PASSIONFRUIT CUPCAKES WITH BLOOD ORANGE SORBET

220g (7oz) butter
230g (7⅓oz) caster sugar
205g (6½oz) eggs
330g (11oz) flour
12g (⅓oz) baking powder
90ml (3fl oz) milk
10g (⅓oz) vanilla bean paste
70g (2⅓oz) passionfruit pulp
1 teaspoon lemon juice

BLOOD ORANGE SORBET
100g (3½oz) caster sugar
500ml (16fl oz) blood orange juice

Preheat oven to 145°C/275°F/Gas mark 1–2.
    Using electric beaters, cream butter and sugar on high speed for 5 to 20 minutes, depending on softness of butter. Mixture should turn from yellow to off-white.
    Add eggs, one at a time, beating between additions. Do not allow mixture to split. Mix until just combined. Do not over mix.
    Sift flour and baking powder together. In a separate bowl, combine milk and vanilla bean paste. Add half the flour mixture and half the milk mixture to the butter mixture. Combine well, then add remaining flour mixture and remaining milk mixture.
    Fold in passionfruit pulp.
    Using an ice-cream scoop, spoon batter into cupcake foils. Bake for 30 minutes, turning tray around once at 15 minutes.

BLOOD ORANGE SORBET
In a saucepan on low heat, combine sugar with just enough juice to cover it.
    Cook until sugar completely dissolves. Allow to cool.
    Add sugar mixture to remaining juice. Refrigerate overnight.
    Use an ice-cream maker to freeze and churn the mixture to make a sorbet.

DECORATION
Scoop ice-cream on top of cupcake. Top with fresh passionfruit.

KUMQUAT CUPCAKES WITH COCONUT ICE-CREAM

1kg (2lb) fresh kumquats, whole
400g (13oz) caster sugar
220g (7oz) butter
230g (7⅓oz) caster sugar
205g (6½oz) eggs
330g (14oz) flour
12g (1oz) baking powder
90ml (3fl oz) milk
10g (⅓oz) vanilla bean paste

First, make candied kumquats: Wash, trim and slice the kumquats. In a large saucepan, cover kumquats with water and bring to a boil. Drain kumquats, set aside to cool and discard the water.

Bring sugar and about 400ml (13fl oz) water to a boil. Remove from heat and set aside to cool. Add kumquats, making sure the sugar syrup covers them completely. Cover with baking paper and poach on low heat until kumquats are translucent.

Preheat oven to 145°C/275°F/Gas Mark 2.

In an electric mixer on high speed, cream butter and sugar until mixture turns from yellow to off-white (between 5 and 20 minutes, depending on softness of butter).

Add eggs, one at a time, beating between additions. Do not allow mixture to split. Mix until just combined. Do not over mix.

Sift flour and baking powder together and, in a separate bowl, combine milk and vanilla bean paste.

Add half the flour mixture and half the milk mixture to the butter mixture. Mix well and then add remaining flour mixture and remaining milk mixture. Fold in about 100g (3½oz) candied kumquat.

Using an ice-cream scoop, spoon mixture into cupcake foils. Bake for 30 minutes, turning tray around once at 15 minutes.

COCONUT ICE-CREAM

500ml (16fl oz) full cream milk
pinch salt
65g (2oz) egg yolk
110g (3½oz) caster sugar
180ml (6fl oz) coconut cream
30g (1oz) molasses

COCONUT ICE-CREAM

Bring milk and salt to a boil. Combine egg and sugar in a large bowl and whisk until sugar dissolves. Stir in coconut cream.

Pour a third of the milk into the egg mixture, whisking continuously so as not to cook the eggs.

Pour the egg yolk mixture back into the saucepan. Cook on low heat, stirring continuously so that it will not stick to the bottom of the saucepan. Cook until mixture is thick enough to coat the back of the spoon.

Remove from heat and place the saucepan in a pot of ice-cold water to stop the cooking process. Add molasses and stir. Refrigerate overnight before processing, using an ice-cream maker.

Serve cupcakes with a scoop of coconut ice-cream.

Remaining candied kumquats can be frozen for several months.

DECORATION

Scoop ice-cream on top of cupcake. Top with kumquat zest.

JUDE'S NAMING DAY PARTY

Hayley and Storm couldn't be more excited at their birth of their baby boy, Jude. Born in Eritrea, the couple is thrilled that Jude has joined their family. His naming day is a celebration of his new life and the new family who cherish him. Friends and family gather over a modern tea party.

SAFFRON AND COCONUT SPARKLE KISSES

MIXTURE 1
150g (5oz) icing sugar
150g (5oz) ground almonds
60g (2oz) egg whites, pasteurised

MIXTURE 2
130g (3⅓oz) caster sugar
pinch saffron thread
40ml (2fl oz) water

MIXTURE 3
60g (2oz) egg whites, pasteurised

MIXTURE 1
Sift icing sugar and ground almonds together. Add egg white and stir to form a paste. Cover paste and set aside.

MIXTURE 2
Ground a pinch of caster sugar and mix together with thread of saffron, to maximise flavour of saffron.
   Heat caster sugar and water in saucepan. Add saffron and bring to the boil.
   Reduce to medium heat and keep cooking until mixture is 118°C/250°F when measured with a food thermometer. Remove from heat and set aside.

MIXTURE 3
Whisk egg whites to form soft peaks using a hand mixer or kitchen mixer.

Preheat oven to 180°C/350°F/Gas mark 4.
   Add the slightly cooled mixture 2 to mixture 3 slowly, mixing continuously. Reduce the speed. Keep whisking while cooling, until the meringue is thick and glossy.
   Add about ¼ of mixture 1 to the combined mixtures 2 and 3. Gently fold together. Add remaining mixture 1 and fold until mixture is just combined.
   Using a piping bag and round nozzle, pipe dollops of mixture a little larger than a 50 cent piece. To make each cookie a similar size, print a stencil of same sized circles and place underneath a piece of baking paper. Using the stencil as a guide, pipe each cookie the same size.
   Bake for 10–15 minutes. Cool.

FILLING
75ml (2⅔fl oz) coconut cream
*150g (5oz) white chocolate, broken
  into pieces*
2 drops coconut essence

FILLING
Bring coconut cream to the boil in a saucepan. Remove from heat and pour into a mixing bowl with white chocolate.

Mix in coconut essence, stir until mixture is smooth and of a spreadable consistency.

Using a piping bag, pipe a dollop of filling on the 'inside' of a cookie and sandwich with a second cookie to create a Sparkle Kiss.

Repeat with remaining cookies and filling.

MANGO JELLY DESSERT SHOT

16 gelatine leaves
150ml (5fl oz) mango syrup
1 fresh mango, cut into little cubes
handful fresh mint leaves

This recipe makes about 20 shots.

Soak gelatine leaves in cold water and set aside. Bring about 1¼L of water to a boil. Pour boiling water into a jug, add mango syrup and set aside.

Once the mango mixture is warm, add the softened gelatine, then stir until gelatine completely dissolves. Fill the bottom of shot glasses with fresh mango, then add the gelatine mango mixture. Refrigerate for at least 4 hours to set. Serve each shot topped with fresh mango and mint leaves.

Clockwise L-R: Chicken Waldorf Sandwich Swirls, Tzatziki and Cucumber Sandwich Slivers, Orange Blossom Sparkle Kisses, Pistachio and Cardamom Cupcakes, Mango Jelly Dessert Shots

TZATZIKI AND CUCUMBER SANDWICH SLIVERS

1 loaf fresh sliced white bread
soft butter
100g (3½oz) tzatziki
1 fresh cucumber, sliced into rounds
sea salt

TZATZIKI
100g (3½oz) greek-style yoghurt
1 teaspoon very finely chopped garlic
handful grated cucumber
juice of half a lemon
salt and pepper to taste

Spread one slice of fresh bread with a very thin layer of butter. Spread one side of each sandwich with tzatziki and top with thin slices of cucumber. Sprinkles some sea salt, to taste. Top with another slice of fresh bread. Repeat with remaining bread.

Cut crusts from sandwiches for beautifully finished slivers.

TZATZIKI
Mix all ingredients together.

CHICKEN WALDORF SANDWICH SWIRLS

100g (3½oz) finely chopped cooked chicken
1 cup finely chopped apple
1 cup finely chopped celery
1 tablespoon mayonnaise
20g (½oz) slivered almonds
salt and pepper to taste
1 loaf fresh sliced white bread
soft butter

Mix together chicken, apple, celery, mayonnaise and almonds until mixture forms a coarse paste. Season to taste.

Remove crusts from bread and spread one slice with a thin layer of butter.

Spread some filling on bread, roll it into a scroll, cut to make swirls and secure with a toothpick.

MINI PISTACHIO AND CARDAMOM CUPCAKES

220g (7oz) butter
230g (7⅓oz) caster sugar
205g (6½oz) eggs
330g (11oz) flour
12g (1oz) baking powder
90ml (3fl oz) milk
10g (⅓oz) vanilla bean paste
30g (1oz) sour cream
40g (1⅓oz) chopped pistachios
7g (⅓oz) ground cardamom

VANILLA FROSTING
115g (4oz) butter
310g (10⅓oz) pure icing sugar
25g (⅔oz) egg white, pasturised
½ teaspoon lemon juice
10g (1oz) vanilla bean extract

Preheat oven to 145°C/275°F/Gas mark 2.

In an electric mixer on high speed, cream butter and sugar until mixture turns from yellow to off-white (between 5 and 20 minutes, depending on softness of butter).

Add eggs, one at a time, beating between additions. Do not allow mixture to split.

Sift flour and baking powder together and, in a separate bowl, combine milk and vanilla bean paste.

Add half the flour mixture, half the milk mixture and half the sour cream to the butter mixture. Mix well, then add remaining flour mixture, milk mixture and sour cream. Fold in pistachios and cardamom powder.

Spoon mixture into mini cupcake foils, about 20g each. Bake for 30 minutes, turning tray around once at 15 minutes.

VANILLA FROSTING
Whip the butter until pale and creamy. Add icing sugar and beat on high speed for a further 5–10 minutes. Add egg whites, lemon juice and vanilla bean extract.
Cream for an additional 3 minutes.

Spread over cooked cupcakes.

ORANGE BLOSSOM SPARKLE KISSES

MIXTURE 1
150g (5oz) icing sugar
150g (5oz) almond meal
60g (2oz) egg white, pasteurised

MIXTURE 2
130g (4oz) caster sugar
5 drops orange blossom syrup
38ml (1⅓ fl oz) water

MIXTURE 3
60g (2oz) egg whites, pasteurised

FILLING
75ml (⅔ fl oz) fresh cream
150g (5oz) dark chocolate
50g (1⅔ oz) ground pistachio
30g (1oz) butter

MIXTURE 1
Sift icing sugar and almond meal together. Add egg white and mix to form a paste. Cover and set aside.

MIXTURE 2:
Heat sugar, orange blossom syrup and water in a saucepan, stirring continuouslyuntil mixture reaches 118°C/250°F when measured with a candy thermometer.

MIXTURE 3
Using electric beaters, whisk egg whites to form soft peaks. Add the slightly cooled mixture 2 slowly, mixing continuously. Reduce the speed and keep whisking while mixture cools, until the meringue is thick and glossy.

Preheat oven to 180°C/350°F/Gas mark 4.
    Add about a quarter of mixture 1 to mixture 3, gently folding together. Add remaining mixture 1 to mixture 3, continuing to fold together. Using a piping bag fitted with a round nozzle, pipe dollops of the mixture a little larger than a 50 cent coin. To make each cookie a similar size, print a stencil of same sized circles and place underneath a piece of baking paper. Using the stencil as a guide, pipe each cookie the same size. Bake for 10–15 minutes. Cool.

FILLING
In a medium saucepan, bring cream to a boil. Remove from heat and pour into a bowl with dark chocolate. Mix in ground pistachios and butter. Stir until mixture is cool and thick.
    Using a piping bag, pipe a dollop of filling on the 'inside' of a cookie and sandwich with a second cookie to create a Sparkle Kiss. Repeat with remaining cookies and filling.

FIDO'S BIRTHDAY

The Walsh family adore their family pooch, Fido. They are baking Fido his very own birthday cake, cupcakes and dog biscuits to share with the other furry friends in their neighbourhood, as they get together, complete with doggie bags—any excuse for a street party.

PUPCAKES

250g (8oz) spelt flour
10g (⅓ oz) baking powder
60ml (2fl oz) vegetable oil
140g (4⅔ oz) eggs
65g (2⅙oz) honey
100ml (3½fl oz) chicken stock
50g (1⅔ oz) canned dog food

Preheat oven to 160°C/325°F/Gas mark 2–3.

Sift spelt flour and baking powder together in a large bowl. In a separate bowl, mix vegetable oil and eggs and add to the flour mixture. Add honey, chicken stock and dog food. Mix well. Bake for 10–15 minutes.

If you like you can finely chop some meaty dog treats. Dip the cooked pupcakes in honey and sprinkle the dog treats over the top.

You can also use carob as a topping.

DOGGIE BIRTHDAY CAKE

210g (6⅔oz) eggs
50g (1⅔oz) wholemeal flour
30g (1oz) spelt flour
30g (1oz) honey
60g (2oz) grated carrot
10g (⅓oz) grated apple
10g (⅓oz) spinach, chopped

Preheat oven to 170°C/335°F/Gas mark 4.
Whisk the eggs in a medium bowl.
In a separate bowl, mix the rest of the ingredients into paste. Fold in one-third of whisked egg, then carefully fold in remaining whisked egg.
Bake for 1 hour. Test cake by inserting a skewer into the middle. If the skewer comes out clean, the cake is cooked.

DOG BISCUITS

150g (5oz) wholemeal flour
75g (2½oz) spelt flour
150g (5oz) oatmeal
pinch baking soda
75g (2½oz) ground dried beef liver
105g (3½oz) egg
195ml (6½fl oz) soy milk

Preheat oven to 160°C/325°F/Gas mark 2–3. Line baking tray with silicone paper.

Place all ingredients except egg and milk in a food processor and blend until smooth.

Add the eggs and the soy milk and process until it forms a dough. On a floured surface, roll out dough to desired thickness. (about 3-4mm/¼in). Using a bone-shaped cookie cutter, cut out shapes in the dough.

Bake for 30 minutes.

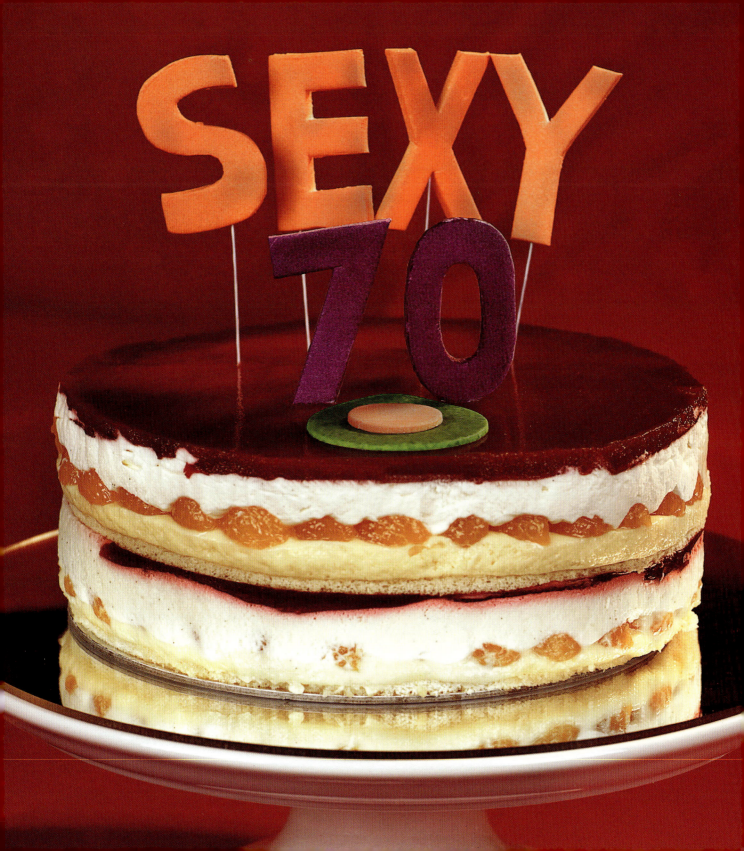

ROCKSTAR GRANDMA

The grandkids came together to bake a 70th birthday cake as racy and flamboyant as their Grandma Martha. She's their superhero—she has been a big part in the lives of each of her four children and 12 grandchildren. Her birthday cake is a tribute to tradition, like the trifle Martha often makes, but with a modern twist.

MANDARIN AND RASPBERRY TRIFLE CELEBRATION CAKE

RASPBERRY JELLY
500ml (16fl oz) raspberry puree, strained
2 teaspoons lemon juice
200g (6½oz) caster sugar
5 gelatine leaves, softened in a bowl of water

SPONGE
180g (6oz) eggs, pasteurised
80g (2⅔oz) caster sugar
45g (1½oz) plain flour, sifted
15g (½oz) cornflour, sifted
25g (⅔oz) unsalted butter, melted
400g (13oz) canned mandarins

MANDARIN CURD
9 eggs, lightly beaten
450g (14½oz) caster sugar
450g (14½oz) mandarin juice
450g (14½oz) butter
5 gelatine leaves, softened in a bowl of water

RASPBERRY JELLY
Heat the raspberry puree and lemon juice over low heat. Add caster sugar and stir. Add soften gelatine leaves and refrigerate until set.

SPONGE:
Preheat oven to 190°C/375°F/Gas Mark 5.
In a large, clean mixing bowl, whisk eggs until pale and fluffy. Add caster sugar gradually. Gently fold in sifted plain flour and cornflour.
Add melted butter and stir until mixture is fully combined. Pour into a 20cm (8in) round cake tin and bake for 8 minutes.

MANDARIN CURD
Combine eggs and half the sugar in a clean, large bowl and whisk until pale and frothy.
Bring mandarin juice and remaining sugar to a boil. As soon as it starts boiling, remove the mixture from heat and pour a third of it into the egg mixture.
Put mandarin juice mixture back onto the stove and continue cooking on low heat, stirring continuously. Once it starts boiling, stop the cooking process by transferring the mixture into a bowl set over another bowl full of ice.
Using a hand mixer or a fork, mix in the butter and softened gelatine leaves.

CHANTILY CREAM
150g (5oz) double cream
1/2 teaspoon vanilla paste
50g (1½oz) caster sugar
1 gelatine leaf, softened in a bowl of water

CHANTILLY CREAM
Whisk double cream and vanilla paste. Add sugar gradually. Melt the gelatine in the microwave for 5-8 seconds. Add one-third of the whipped cream to the gelatine and mix well. Pour the gelatine mixture into the whipped cream mixture and mix well.

To assemble the cake, cut the sponge into two rounds. Pipe the mandarin curd on the base layer, then top with drained mandarin wedges.

Spread chantilly cream over mandarins, smoothen then refrigerate until set.

Top with raspberry jelly and repeat with remaining cake layer and the remaining ingredients.

FASHION FORWARD

It's fashion week. Designers have spent sleepless nights in preparation and impossibly gorgeous models are gathered to showcase the season's lastest must-have pieces. While the gowns are on show, it's the mini skinny cupcakes that the crowds are oohing and aahing over!

FRUIT SKEWERS WITH LAVENDER DIPPING SAUCE

strawberries
blueberries
kiwi fruit
(This is what we have used, feel free to use the fruit of your choice)

LAVENDER DIPPING SAUCE
250ml (8fl oz) water
250g (8oz) sugar
3 drops edible lavender oil

Boil water and sugar together until sugar has dissolved. Transfer to serving bowl, add drops of lavender oil and stir.

Thread whole strawberries, blueberries and wedges of kiwi fruit (or pieces of the fruit of your choice) onto wooden or metal skewers.

THE SKINNY CUPCAKE

360g (12oz) egg whites, pasteurised
pinch cream of tartar
pinch salt
340g (11½oz) natural sugar substitute*
40g (1⅓oz) plain flour, sifted
10g (⅓oz) vanilla extract
1 teaspoon lemon juice
½ teaspoon lemon zest

STRAWBERRY FILLING
300g (10oz) strawberries
60ml (2fl oz) water

Preheat oven to 160°C/325°F/Gas mark 2–3.
   Using electric beaters, whisk egg whites, cream of tartar and salt at high speed. Slowly add sugar substitute. Whisk until soft peaks form. Sift flour twice and add to the meringue. Gently fold in vanilla extract, lemon juice and lemon zest.
   Line a mini-cupcake tray with paper cases. Fill with about 20g (⅔oz) of mixture. Bake about 25 minutes or until cupcakes are brown on top and spring back when pressed lightly.

STRAWBERRY FILLING
Chop strawberries finely. Combine them with about 60ml (2fl oz) of water in a saucepan. heat for about 15 minutes, stirring regularly.
   Once cupcakes are cooked and while still warm, use a small syringe to 'inject each cake with about 3g (1/10oz) of strawberry filling.
   Dollop with whipped cream or dust with icing sugar if desired.

*There are a number of natural sugar replacements, such as Stevia. We use Nativa..

PATCH OF GRASS

Troy, Mary and their group of friends have found the perfect patch of grass at a harbourside park, to while away a lazy Sunday afternoon. Everyone brought along their favourite gourmet treat for the group to graze on: they've picked through cheese and crackers, sliced meats and crusty bread; now it's time for sweet treats. Sarah and Darren baked cupcakes, just perfect for an afternoon in the sunshine.

LAMINGTON CUPCAKES

160g (5⅓oz) eggs
110g (3⅔oz) caster sugar
1 teaspoon vanilla paste
115g (3¾oz) plain flour, sifted
30g (1oz) butter
45ml (1¾fl oz) milk

DARK CHOCOLATE GANACHE
100g (3½oz) pure cream
125g (4oz) dark chocolate
35g (1⅙oz) butter
50g (1½oz) shredded coconut

Preheat oven to 170°C/350°F/Gas mark 4.
 Using electric beaters, whisk eggs, sugar and vanilla until mixture is fluffy and pale. Once mixture is thick enough to coat the back of a spoon, fold flour in. Melt the butter and add milk. Stir to combine, then add butter mixture to egg mixture. Using an ice-cream scoop, spoon batter into cupcake foils and bake for about 15 or 20 minutes.

DARK CHOCOLATE GANACHE
 In a saucepan on medium heat, bring cream to the boil. Remove from heat and pour into a medium bowl with chocolate.
 Add butter and stir until melted.
 Dip cupcake in ganache and roll in shredded coconut.

MACADAMIA AND WATTLESEED CUPCAKES

220g (7oz) butter
230g (7⅓oz) caster sugar
205g (6½oz) eggs
330g (11oz) flour
12g (⅓oz) baking powder
90ml (3fl oz) milk
10g (⅓oz) vanilla bean paste
50g (1½oz) chopped macadamia nuts
10g (⅓oz) wattleseed

LEMON FROSTING
115g (4oz) butter
310g (10⅓oz) pure icing sugar
25g (¾oz) egg white, pasteurised
8ml lemon juice
several drops lemon oil

Preheat oven to 145°C/275°F/Gas mark 2.

In an electric mixer on high speed, cream butter and sugar until mixture turns from yellow to off-white (between 5 and 20 minutes, depending on softness of butter).

Add eggs, one at a time, beating between additions. Do not allow mixture to split. Sift flour and baking powder together and, in a separate bowl, combine milk and vanilla bean paste.

Add half the flour mixture and half the milk mixture to the butter mixture. Mix well, then add remaining flour mixture and milk mixture. Fold in nuts and wattleseed.

Using an ice-cream scoop, spoon mixture into cupcake foils. Bake for 30 minutes, turning tray around once at 15 minutes.

LEMON FROSTING
Whip the butter until slightly pale and creamy. Add icing sugar and beat on high speed for further 5–10 minutes.

Add egg whites, lemon juice and lemon oil. Cream for an additional 3 minutes.

DECORATION
Spread frosting over cooked cupcakes. Top with half a macadamia nut.

PAVLOVA CUPCAKES

ITALIAN MERINGUE FILLING
35g (1oz) egg white, pasteurised
90ml (3fl oz) water
25g (1fl oz) caster sugar

PAVLOVA CUPCAKES
220g (7oz) butter
230g (7⅓oz) caster sugar
205g (6½oz) eggs
330g (11oz) flour
12g (⅓oz) baking powder
90ml (3fl oz) milk
10g (⅓oz) vanilla bean paste

ITALIAN MERINGUE FILLING
In a mixing bowl, whisk egg whites until frothy.

In a saucepan over medium heat, heat water and sugar to 118°C/250°F (use a sugar thermometer). Once the sugar syrup reaches this temperature, pour it into the egg whites and mix on low speed.

Gradually increase the speed until mixture is thick and glossy.

PAVLOVA CUPCAKES
Preheat oven to 145°C/275°F/Gas Mark 2.

Using an electric mixer on high speed, cream butter and sugar until mixture turns from yellow to off-white (between 5 and 20 minutes, depending on softness of butter).

Add eggs, one at a time, beating between additions. Do not allow mixture to split.

Sift together flour and baking powder. In a separate bowl, combine milk and vanilla bean paste. Add half the flour mixture and half the milk mixture to the butter mixture.

Add remaining flour mixture then remaining milk mixture. Mix well.

Using an ice-cream scoop, spoon mixture into cupcake foils. Bake for 30 minutes, turning tray around once at 15 minutes.

When cupcakes are cool enough to touch, use an apple corer to remove centre of cupcakes. Fill each cupcake with two teaspoons of Italian meringue. Replace a small piece of cake over the top of filling to seal.

PAVLOVA CRUST
90g egg white, pasteurised
270g caster sugar
3 drops vinegar
27g corn flour

BUTTER CREAM
115g (3¾oz) butter
310g (10⅓oz) pure icing sugar
25g (⅔oz) egg white, pasturised
3 drops lemon juice
10g ($^{11}/_{10}$oz) vanilla bean extract

PAVLOVA CRUST
Whisk egg white with a third of the sugar in a bowl set over a saucepan of boiling water until the sugar totally dissolves. Add vinegar and keep whisking.
Add another third of caster sugar, while whisking . Then add combined cornflour and remaining caster sugar. Whisk until just combined.
Pipe the meringue on to a baking tray lined with baking paper. Bake at 150°C/300°F/Gas mark 2 for 15 minutes. Set aside to cool. Once it is completely cool, bake again for another 15 minutes or until it is crusty.

BUTTER CREAM
To make the icing, whip the butter until pale and creamy. Add icing sugar and beat on high speed for further 5–10 minutes.
Add egg whites, lemon juice and vanilla bean extract. Cream an additional 3 minutes.

DECORATION
Top each cupcake with a dollop of buttercream. Sprinkle with pieces of pavlova crust. Decorate with fresh fruit of your choice.

SPOOKY STUFF

Perhaps this annual ritual stemmed from spooky stuff. However, Halloween now stands for fun times in hilarious costumes and buckets full of candy. Alex and Brodie are off to their friend's party, dressed as vampires, with a plate of seriously spooky cupcakes as a seasonal treat for the host.

PUMPKIN SPICE CUPCAKES

220g (7oz) butter
230g (7⅓oz) caster sugar
205g (6½oz) eggs
330g (11oz) flour
12g (⅓oz) baking powder
90ml (3fl oz) milk
10g (⅓oz) vanilla bean paste
200g (6oz) mashed butternut pumpkin
½ teaspoon ground nutmeg
½ teaspoon ground cinnamon
½ teaspoon mixed spice

CREAM CHEESE FROSTING
115g (3¾oz) butter
25g (⅔oz) cream cheese, softened
310g (10⅔oz) pure icing sugar
25g (⅔oz) egg white, pasteurised
1 teaspoon lemon juice
10g (⅓oz) vanilla bean extract
pinch salt

Preheat oven to 145°C/275°F/Gas mark 2.
 In an electric mixer on high speed, cream butter and sugar until mixture turns from yellow to off-white (between 5 and 20 minutes, depending on softness of butter).
 Add eggs, one at a time, beating between additions. Do not allow mixture to split. Sift flour and baking powder together and, in a separate bowl, combine milk and vanilla bean paste.
 Add half the flour mixture and half the milk mixture to the butter mixture. Mix well then add remaining flour mixture and milk mixture. Fold in pumpkin and spices.
 Using an ice-cream scoop, spoon mixture into cupcake foils and bake for 30 minutes, turning tray around once at 15 minutes.

CREAM CHEESE FROSTING
Whip the butter and cream cheese until pale and creamy. Add icing sugar and cream on high speed for 5–10 minutes.
 Add egg whites, lemon juice, vanilla bean extract and salt. Cream for an additional 3 minutes.
 Spread over cooked cupcakes.

DECORATION
Top with sugar ghost shapes coloured black or orange.

MAPLE SYRUP AND PECAN CUPCAKES

220g (7oz) butter
230g (7⅓oz) caster sugar
205g (6½oz) eggs
330g (11oz) flour
12g (⅓oz) baking powder
90ml (3fl oz) milk
10g (⅓oz) vanilla bean paste
80g (2⅔oz) crushed pecans
30g (1oz) maple syrup

MAPLE SYRUP FROSTING
115g (4oz) butter
310g (10⅓oz) pure icing sugar
25g (⅔oz) egg white, pasteurised
1 teaspoon lemon juice
10g (⅓oz) maple syrup

Preheat oven to 145°C/275°F/Gas mark 2.

In an electric mixer on high speed, cream butter and sugar until mixture turns from yellow to off-white (between 5 and 20 minutes, depending on softness of butter).

Add eggs, one at a time, beating between additions. Do not allow mixture to split. Sift flour and baking powder together and, in a separate bowl, combine milk and vanilla bean paste.

Add half the flour mixture and half the milk mixture to the butter mixture. Mix well, then add remaining flour mixture and milk mixture. Fold in pecans and maple syrup.

Using an ice-cream scoop, spoon mixture into cupcake foils and bake for 30 minutes, turning tray around once at 15 minutes.

MAPLE SYRUP FROSTING
Whip the butter until pale and creamy. Add icing sugar and beat on high speed for further 5–10 minutes.

Add egg whites, lemon juice and maple syrup. Cream for an additional 3 minutes.

Spread over cooked cupcakes.

DECORATION
Top with sugar ghost shapes, coloured black or orange.

SPRING CARNIVAL

It's Spring Carnival at the Royal Racecourse. Jockeys are in their vibrant colours. Glistening racehorses are taking their places at the starting gates. Champagne is flowing, bets are being placed, ladies and gentlemen are dressed in their finery. Bite-size berry cupcakes are the perfect complement to spring time festivities.

BITE-SIZE BERRY CUPCAKES

220g (7oz) butter
230g (7⅓oz) caster sugar
205g (6½oz) eggs
330g (11oz) flour
12g (⅓oz) baking powder
90ml (3fl oz) milk
10g (⅓oz) vanilla bean paste
100g (3½oz) chopped berries*
25g (⅔oz) berry syrup

BERRY SCENTED FROSTING
115g (4oz) butter
310g (3⅓oz) pure icing sugar
25g (⅔oz) egg white, pasturised
½ teaspoon lemon juice
1 teaspoon berry syrup

Preheat oven to 145°C/275°F/Gas mark 2.

In an electric mixer on high speed, cream butter and sugar until mixture turns from yellow to off-white (between 5 and 20 minutes, depending on softness of butter).

Add eggs, one at a time, beating between additions. Do not allow mixture to split. Sift flour and baking powder together and, in a separate bowl, combine milk and vanilla bean paste.

Add half the flour mixture and half the milk mixture to the butter mixture. Mix well, then add remaining flour mixture and milk mixture. Fold in chopped berries and berry syrup.

Add remaining sifted flour and baking powder, then remaining milk mixture.

Spoon teaspoons of the mixture into mini cupcake foils. Bake for 15 minutes.

BERRY SCENTED FROSTING
Whip the butter until pale and creamy. Add icing sugar and beat on high speed for further 5–10 minutes.

Add egg whites, lemon juice and syrup. Cream for an additional 3 minutes.

Spread over cooked cupcakes.

* Strawberries, blueberries or rasberries can be used for this recipe.

LITTLE BOY BLUE

It's Josh's third birthday. Simplicity is the key to this gathering with friends, family and lots of little tots. There were many fabulous photos of the children licking the icing from their cupcakes and smearing it onto every corner of their tiny faces.

AFTERNOON DELIGHT CUPCAKES

220g (7oz) butter
230g (7⅓oz) caster sugar
205g (6½oz) eggs
330g (11oz) flour
12g (⅓oz) baking powder
90ml (3fl oz) milk
10g (⅓oz) vanilla bean paste
10g (⅓oz) ground cinnamon
30ml (3fl oz) apple juice concentrate

VANILLA FROSTING
115g (4oz) butter
310g (11oz) pure icing sugar
25g (⅔oz) egg white (pasteurised)
½ teaspoon lemon juice
10g (⅓oz) vanilla bean extract

Preheat oven to 145°C/275°F/Gas mark 2.

In an electric mixer on high speed, cream butter and sugar until mixture turns from yellow to off-white (between 5 and 20 minutes, depending on softness of butter).

Add eggs, one at a time, beating between additions. Do not allow mixture to split. Mix until just combined. Do not over mix.

Sift flour and baking powder together and, in a separate bowl, combine milk and vanilla bean paste.

Add half the flour mixture and half the milk mixture to the butter mixture. Mix well, then add remaining flour mixture and milk mixture. Fold in cinnamon and apple juice concentrate. Mix well.

Use an ice-cream scoop to spoon mixture into cupcake foils. Bake for 30 minutes, turning tray around once at 15 minutes.

VANILLA FROSTING
Whip the butter until pale and creamy. Add icing sugar and beat on high speed for further 5–10 minutes.

Add egg whites, lemon juice and vanilla bean extract. Beat for an additional 3 minutes.

DECORATION
Use a piping bag with large round nozzle to pipe frosting on top of cooked cupcakes.

Make flags from coloured paper and mount on toothpicks.

Great designs on your cakes and cupcakes depends upon sourcing the right equipment and having a handle on the technique.

CLASSIC SPARKLE FINISH

Using a palette knife, follow a few simple steps for the classic Sparkle finish. First, generously spread buttercream over the top of the cupcake. Smooth buttercream for a flat surface.

Smooth the sides of the cupcake with buttercream, using your palette knife at a 90 degree angle to the cake

Dip the palette knife in very hot water. Smooth the top of the cupcake and the sides, to achieve a glossy smooth finish.

SUGAR SHAPES

Using Ready To Roll fondant (RTR), a rolling pin and some icing sugar or cornflour sprinkled to avoid sticking, roll RTR to several millimetres thickness.

RTR can be coloured to any shade, using food colouring. Your specialty cake decorating store will have a range of colours and strength of colour is determined by amount of colouring added.

Using a cutter, cut a shape from the rolled RTR. Allow to dry and harden. Use shape to decorate cupcake.

Using a round cutter, cut a circle the size of your cupcake from rolled RTR. This can be used to entirely cover the cupcake and smoothed over, before drying, while RTR is still pliable.

MOUNTING SUGAR SHAPES ON WIRE

After cutting desired sugar shape from instructions above, use a piece of sturdy wire. Ensure the sugar shape is reasonable thick to enable the wire to be inserted. Allow the sugar shape to dry while lying flat. Once dry, the wire can be stuck into the cake or cupcake, just like a candle.

EDIBLE GLITTER

Edible glitter gives the bling to many a Sparkle cupcake. Obtain your edible glitter from a specialty cake decorating supply store. Using a dab of water on a sugar shape allows you to dust the decoration with a little glitter. Voila!

Edible glitter can be dusted over the top of wet ganache or buttercream for a sparkly finish.

CHOCOLATE TRANSFERS

Different designs and patterns for chocolate transfers are available for specialty cake decorating stores.

  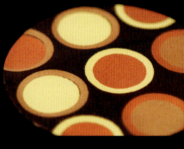

Melt chocolate, either very slowly in the microwave, or over bain marie.

Spread melted chocolate over chocolate transfer. Allow to set. Cut desired shape, using cutter, from chocolate.

PIPED BUTTERCREAM

A piping bag can be used to pipe buttercream on top of your cupcake. Use your bench to practice your piping before taking on your cake.

By changing the size of the nozzle, more intricate designs can be piped.

ABOUT THE AUTHOR

Kathryn Sutton, Founder and Director of Sparkle Cupcakery believes 'the more cupcakes in the world, the better!'. Originally from Sydney, she spent a decade offshore, living and working in Singapore and then New York.

Having started in the world of elegant hotels, Kathryn has come back to her origins, serving people exquisite food and beverages in stunning surroundings. Living in New York City, dubbed the worldwide hub of cupcakes, with numerous cupcake bakeries dotted throughout Manhattan, the idea of hatching a cupcakery back in Sydney was born. Sparkle Cupcakery brings together many ideas from great brands seen overseas and plenty of Australian inspiration.

The most important aspect for Kathryn, as Founder and Director, is the experience that customers get from the entire team when visiting Sparkle. It's beyond a store. It's every element, from the cakes, the service, the décor, the stunning packaging and the way they conduct business. It's about every element coming together to provide each customer with a great feeling when they walk away, cupcakes in hand.

Published in 2011 by
New Holland Publishers (Australia) Pty Ltd
Sydney • Auckland • London • Cape Town

www.newholland.com.au

1/66 Gibbes Street Chatswood NSW 2067 Australia
218 Lake Road Northcote Auckland New Zealand
86 Edgware Road London W2 2EA United Kingdom
80 McKenzie Street Cape Town 8001 South Africa

Copyright © 2011 in text: Kathryn Sutton
Copyright © 2011 in images: Karen Watson
Copyright © 2011 New Holland Publishers (Australia) Pty Ltd

All rights reserved. No part of this publication may be reproduced, stored in a retrieval system or transmitted, in any form or by any means, electronic, mechanical, photocopying, recording or otherwise, without the prior written permission of the publishers and copyright holders.

A record of this is held at the National Library of Australia.

ISBN: 9781742570723

Publisher: Diane Jardine
Publishing manager: Lliane Clarke
Project editor: Rochelle Fernandez
Proofreader: Nina Paine
Designer: Emma Gough
Photography: Karen Watson
Styling: Kathy McKinnon
Production manager: Olga Dementiev
Printer: Toppan Leefung Printing Limited (China)

The publisher and the author would like to thank the following businesses for their kind support:

Space 84 O'Riordan Street, Alexandria www.spacefurniture.com.au
Chee Soon & Fitzgerald 387 Crown Street, Surry Hills www.cheesoonfitzgerald.com
Paddo Pets 2 Boundary Street, Paddington www.paddopets.com.au
Niki Shoes 401 Crown Street, Surry Hills www.nikishoes.com.au
Empire Beads 80 Cooper Street, Surry Hills www.empirebeads.com.au